To Travel is to Live

journal belongs to...

© 2016 Ranch House Press
All rights reserved. Printed in the United States of America.

www.annettebridges.com

ISBN: 978-1-946371-02-7

Journal Prompts

To Travel is to Live

1. Peter Pan said, "To live will be an awfully big adventure." What does this mean to you?
2. What is one of your best trips ever? Who were you with, where did you travel to, what were some of the sights that you saw?
3. Is travel stressful for you? What would you have to do to take the stress out of traveling? A closer airport? Calmer family members? Your own jet? Detail a stress-free traveling experience.
4. Write about a driving road trip that you've had. Who was there, where were you going, what seedy rest stops did you go to along the way? Are there driving road trips you want to take?
5. Write about a trip that involved getting stranded or interrupted? Flight canceled? Car broke down? Blizzard? Hurricane? Spend the night at an airport? Or if this has never happened to you before, imagine how you would feel or react if it did.
6. If money or time were not a concern, where would you go?
7. Have you fallen in love with a destination, new tradition or new language? Describe your love and what you love about it.
8. Is it possible to get lost in the right direction? What does this mean to you?
9. Tell a story about someone you've traveled with or people you have met on your travels.
10. If someone were to make the same trip as one you've loved, what tips and recommendations would you share with other travelers?
11. Think about foods you have tried in your travels. Is there a favorite that you would love to have again? Describe in full sensory detail.
12. What is the most amazing moment that is forever embedded in your travel memories?
13. Scrapbook your favorite travel photos and record your memories of what was happening when the picture was taken.
14. Make a list of ten memorable travels in your life. Jot down a few notes about why each is memorable.
15. Make a list of ten places you would like to travel to and note what you hope to experience or see when you go.
16. What have you learned about yourself while traveling?
17. "You must go on adventures to find out where you truly belong." What does this mean to you?
18. Make a list of songs you would include on a road trip sound track.
19. Compare a vacation setting to your regular daily life setting. What do you enjoy about each. What is it about your vacation setting that you would like to bring back to your daily life? What can your vacation self suggest to your personal self to incorporate more fulfillment into each day?
20. Go somewhere local you've never been before. Lake, park, coffee shop, restaurant, museum, etc. Record what you see before you. Describe the scene in detail. How you feel – the emotions your setting stirs within you.
21. Play travel roulette. Write on several slips of paper places you want to explore and put in a little bucket. Pick one and begin planning your trip in your journal.
22. Save your packing list! Create a packing list of items you would generally take with you no matter where you went.
23. Fill in the blank: Advice I would like to give myself before my next trip is …
24. "Travel is the only thing you buy, that makes you richer." Write about a trip where you learned a grand life lesson or that changed your life in some way.
25. Have you ever traveled alone? If you were to plan a future trip alone, where would you want to go, where would you stay, what would you do?
26. Cut out magazine photos of settings you dream of experiencing.
27. Start a collection of quotations about traveling that inspire you.
28. "Let's wander where the wifi is weak." If you did this, where would you love to go?
29. What would be a new adventure to you?
30. Where have you traveled that you felt the happiest? What was it about the location or experience that you think contributed the most to your joy?

color your world

ABOUT the CREATOR

Annette Bridges is an author, publisher and women's retreat host on a mission to help every woman realize her story is extraordinary, valuable and noteworthy.

She has published the *Color Your World Journal Series* and formed a journal club to provide community, support and tools for women to record their ideas, feelings, experiences, memories and all the important details of their lives.

Before writing books and publishing journals and coloring books, this former public school and homeschool educator spent a decade writing hundreds of helpful, instructive, and light-hearted columns published by Texas newspapers, parenting magazines, websites and bloggers.

Annette lives on a Texas cattle ranch with her husband John, dachshund Lady and lots of cows. She can drive a tractor but only if wearing a fresh coat of lipstick and it's not her pedicure day!

You can learn more about Annette's books and products, blogs and videos as well as her women's retreats and other events at www.annettebridges.com.

Look for her on social media, too!

MESSAGE from the PUBLISHER

The *Color Your World Journal Series* is a pathway to self-discovery. It's where you write notes to yourself. Be your own cheerleader. Give yourself encouragement. Tell yourself what you're grateful for. Celebrate you!

There are countless reasons to keep a journal including collecting favorite recipes, listing goals and celebrating every experience and every one that's near and dear to you. A journal provides a home for the memories and lessons learned that you never want to forget.

Why a niche journal?

If you're anything like me, you have a journal (or even two or three journals) where you write anything and everything about anything and everything. My challenge comes when trying to find something I've written. I flip and flip through the pages of my two, three or four journals trying to find whatever it is. I never remember which journal I wrote down my whatever's!!

The solution? A niche journal! A journal that has a specific focus and theme! A journal where you can record your ideas, inspirations and things you want to remember in the appropriate journal.

Why big unlined paper?

Because big unlined paper is needed to record big ideas, dreams and memories! You need room to grow, stretch and expand. You need space to think beyond the confines of what you've always done, to pursue new dreams, discover your power and reimagine your purpose again and again. You need pages without lines and limitations to reconnect with your creative, perfectly imperfect self.

Plus, big unlined paper gives you space for more than words. You have plenty of room to doodle, draw or post photographs and clippings, too.

Why color is important?

When you journal, use colored pens and markers! Your world doesn't happen in black and white. Your life should be lived and written about in many colors. Even dark and sad memories feel lighter and brighter when told in color.

Journaling in color affects your mood and perception of your world. Colors evoke calm, cheer and comfort. Using color can lift your spirit and inspire your imagination. You may be surprised by all the beautiful benefits from adding more color into your life story.

When journaling, give yourself time to listen to your heart and reflect. Breathe in the moments. Feel. Be quiet. Let yourself be totally and thoroughly present with your thoughts. Let your heart transform you and teach you new insights. Open your mind to consider new ideas and possibilities. You may find that what your heart teaches will be life changing.

www.ingramcontent.com/pod-product-compliance
Lightning Source LLC
Chambersburg PA
CBHW051253110526
44588CB00025B/2980